Things I've Had To Learn
Over And Over And Over
(Plus a Few Minor Discoveries)

Things I've Had To Learn
Over And Over And Over
(Plus a Few Minor Discoveries)

Charles M. Schulz

Holt, Rinehart and Winston **New York**

To Dr. Ward Wick,
who thinks of good titles

Published by Holt, Rinehart and Winston,
383 Madison Avenue, New York, New York 10017.

Published simultaneously in Canada by Holt, Rinehart and
Winston of Canada, Limited.

Library of Congress Catalog Card Number: 84-80292

ISBN: 0-03-000742-9

First Edition

Printed in the United States of America
1 3 5 7 9 10 8 6 4 2

ISBN 0-03-000742-9

Things I've Had To Learn
Over And Over And Over
(Plus a Few Minor Discoveries)

Chatter is not conversation.

Don't waste too much effort
on an English theme if
there isn't going to be
any media coverage.

**Never jog on a golf course.
You could run into a
string of double bogeys.**

The early bird need not pursue the worm when he can order pizza at midnight.

**A hug is better than
all the theology in the world.**

Candy bars are like years.
We're paying more,
but they're getting shorter.

How sharper than
a serpent's tooth
is a sister's "See?"

**Stocking caps are great . . .
if you don't mind getting
your ears wrinkled.**

It's hard to tell everybody
they can go home
if nobody shows up.

**If you don't got it,
you don't have it.**

Never try to visit the tree where you were born.

**Small trophies are
for hollow victories.**

You can't discuss something
with someone whose
arguments are too narrow.

No one should be expected
to solve a math problem
that has a "twelve" in it.

**The only time a dog
gets complimented is
when he doesn't do anything.**

**If they go on a cruise and
don't get kissed,
it's always the travel agent's fault.**

I'm not good at names,
but I never forget a slight.

Always get off the ice before the Zamboni starts.

**You can't sulk in
a dining room chair.**

You can't eat compliments.

Always turn out your closet light. Otherwise, you'll get up some morning and find you can't start your closet.

**Never complain about
the weather. . . . Whimper,
but don't complain.**

If they ask you to convert Fahrenheit to Celsius, remember that it's easier just to put on a sweater.

Seasick is bad,
carsick is bad . . .
nestsick is the worst.

**Education can be painful
if you get your finger
caught in your binder.**

**The pen may be mightier
than the sword,
but not a sister's mouth.**

What are friends for if you can't forget them?

If your life is going by too fast, maybe someone pushed the fast-forward button.

If life seems to have
more questions than answers,
try to be the one
who asks the questions.

It's hard to sleep at night
if you're worried that a
ten-pound frog from Southern
Cameroon may come and
jump on your stomach.

Fat is not mature.

When you're waiting for your supper, a watched back door never opens.

It's too late to crawl back into the egg.

Don't worry about the world coming to an end today. It's already tomorrow in Australia.

**Life is like a
ten-speed bicycle.
Most of us have
gears we never use.**

When it's hot in the classroom, and you fall asleep at your desk, your math paper sticks to your head.

Eating in the rain tends to cool down your pizza.

If life is like a baseball game, try to find out how many innings they're playing.

**School can be very helpful,
but, like a prescription,
should be taken only as directed.**

They say we all have to
deal with the law from
the very day we're born . . .
so sue a baby!

If you're not sure she loves you,
blockhead her out of your mind.

The only real way to look younger is not to be born so soon.

You know it's cold when you
can hear your feet coughing.

Those who believe in the "balance of nature" are those who don't get eaten.

**Most of us have to be
satisfied if we just
look good at a distance.**

Never neglect writing letters of appreciation to someone who has been good to you.

Dear Supper Dish,

You can't survive by sucking the juice from a wet mitten.

**Birthday presents from
Grandma are a problem.
The sweaters are too big
and the money is too small.**

When lawyers say, "*sine mora*,"
they mean "without delay,"
but lawyers say a lot of things.

When you leave for the afternoon, be careful how your secretary signs your letters.

S/w
(Dictated, but not worth reading)

Life can be as full as a grocery cart . . . unless you have six items or less.

To avoid getting sick while traveling, be careful what you eat, and stay home.

**Decorate your home.
It gives the illusion that
your life is more interesting
than it really is.**

It's not difficult to find
your way in the wilderness if
you remember that Hollywood is
in the West and the moon
is always over Hollywood.

A Christmas story should always have a character in it whom everyone can love.

Tiny Jim

What's good about hiking is there's no "offside."

Yelling at your brother three times is one more than the recommended daily allowance.

If you're busy, you don't have to answer the phone, and sleeping is busy.

**Try to avoid
long good-byes.**

Be thankful and drink
a toast to the man who
invented the roof.

**And when all else fails,
blame it on the media.**